MEET
GEORGE WASHINGTON

For Jean, Harriet, and Lorraine Nelson

First paperback edition, 1989

Text copyright © 1964 by Random House, Inc. Illustrations copyright © 1989 by Stephen Marchesi. All rights reserved under International and Pan-American Copyright Conventions. Published in the United States by Random House, Inc., New York, and simultaneously in Canada by Random House of Canada Limited, Toronto.

Library of Congress Cataloging-in-Publication Data:
Heilbroner, Joan. Meet George Washington / written by Joan Heilbroner ; illustrated by Stephen Marchesi. p. cm.—(Step-up biographies) SUMMARY: Highlights the life of the first president, known as the father of his country.
ISBN: 0-394-81965-9 (pbk.); 0-394-91965-3 (lib. bdg.)
1. Washington, George, 1732–1799—Juvenile literature. 2. Presidents—United States—Biography—Juvenile literature. [1. Washington, George, 1732–1799. 2. Presidents.] I. Marchesi, Stephen, ill. II. Title. III. Series. E312.66.H4 1989
973.4'1'0924—dc19 [B] [92] 88-19067

Manufactured in the United States of America 1 2 3 4 5 6 7 8 9 0

MEET
GEORGE WASHINGTON

★ ★ ★ ★

By Joan Heilbroner
Illustrated by Stephen Marchesi

STEP-UP BOOKS
Random House New York

CONTENTS

1

MEET
GEORGE WASHINGTON

George Washington was the first president of the United States of America. He was a great American general. Many people think he was the greatest American who ever lived.

But George Washington was not born an American. He was born an Englishman.

George Washington was born in Virginia in the year 1732.

In 1732, Virginia was an English colony. It belonged to England. And it was ruled by the king of England. The people of Virginia felt that they were English.

There were 13 English colonies in America when Washington was a boy. Each colony had its own part of the land. Each had its own churches and its own soldiers. And each had its own kind of farms.

In Virginia the farmers grew tobacco. They had slaves to do the work. And tobacco made many Virginia farmers rich.

George Washington's father was a rich Virginia farmer. In many ways he lived like an English gentleman. He wore English clothes. He rode English horses. He had fine things from England in his house. He even sent his older sons to school in England. He wanted them to learn the ways of English gentlemen.

George's father owned about 50 slaves. And he owned three farms on the Potomac River. George Washington lived on all these farms as a little boy. But when George was seven, the Washingtons moved to a new farm on the Rappahannock River. They called it Ferry Farm.

2

READING, WRITING, AND RULES

Soon after the Washingtons moved to Ferry Farm, George went to school. His father did not send him to school in England, like his brothers.

George learned reading and arithmetic and handwriting. He worked hard on his writing. He wanted it to look good.

George learned writing by copying from books. He had a book of rules for young gentlemen. He copied all the rules.

"Sit not when others stand," wrote George. "Sleep not when others speak." And "Spit not in the fire."

These were the rules that young gentlemen learned in those days. There were 110 of them!

George learned many things outside of school too. He learned to fish. He learned to swim. And he learned how to use a gun. He liked to hunt for ducks along the river.

George was a tall, strong boy. He became good at all kinds of sports. Before

long, he could run faster than any of his friends. And he soon learned to ride a horse better than anyone his age. In a few years he would be called the best rider in Virginia.

When George was ten, his oldest

brother, Lawrence, came back to Virginia to live. Lawrence was a soldier. He had gone to fight for the English in a war with Spain.

Lawrence talked about the battles he had fought in. He talked about far-off lands. George liked to hear about these things.

George looked up to his soldier brother. And Lawrence liked his little brother George. They did many things together.

This was a happy year for George Washington. But the next year was a sad one. When George was 11, his father died.

3

GEORGE GROWS UP

George was only a boy when his father died. But he grew up fast. When he was 14, he was as strong as a man. He wanted to go to sea. But his mother did not want him to go to sea. And George soon found other work to do.

George became a surveyor. A surveyor measures land and makes maps of land.

There was a great need for surveyors in the colonies. Many farmers were buying new land in the west of Virginia. So George made many trips to the West.

Few people lived in the west of Virginia. There were miles of woods between farms. George often had to sleep in the woods. He had to shoot wild ducks for his supper. He cooked them over a fire.

This was not like the easy life at Ferry Farm. But George liked this kind of living. And he soon learned to be a good surveyor.

In these years George went often to see his brother Lawrence. Lawrence had married soon after his father died. He lived on a farm called Mount Vernon.

Life was gay at Mount Vernon. There were many parties and balls. George wore fine new coats and white silk stockings. He danced with the young ladies of

Virginia. George Washington loved to dance!

George had many happy times at Mount Vernon. But when George was 20, Lawrence became ill.

George took Lawrence to the island of Barbados. He hoped Lawrence would get well there. But he never got well again. He came home to Mount Vernon to die.

4

A YOUNG SOLDIER

Soon after Lawrence died, George Washington became a soldier in the army of Virginia.

There was trouble at that time between the English and the French.

The French colonists lived up north in Canada and along the Mississippi River.

The English colonists lived along the Atlantic Ocean. Between the French and the English, there were many miles of land.

There were no towns or farms on this land. There were not even any roads. For miles and miles, there was nothing but woods and fields. This was the land where the Indians lived. It was a great, wild land. People called it the wilderness.

The wilderness was a land rich in furs. All through the wilderness there were animals with fine fur coats. Indians hunted these animals.

The Indians sold the animals' furs to the French and to the English.

Who owned this rich land of furs? The English felt it belonged to England. But the French said it belonged to France.

In 1753 the French began coming down the rivers from Canada. They began to take over the wilderness. The governor of Virginia knew that something had to be done.

The next spring, the governor sent 200 Virginia soldiers into the wilderness. He sent George Washington to lead them.

Deep in the woods, Washington and his men found 50 French soldiers. Washington felt the soldiers had no right to be there!

There was a fight that day in the wilderness. Nine French soldiers were killed. This was the first fighting that Washington had seen. But he was not afraid. George Washington was a brave soldier.

That year there was more fighting in the wilderness. Soon the fighting grew into a war.

5

THE FRENCH AND INDIAN WAR

In 1755 the king sent 2,000 English soldiers to Virginia. They came to help the Virginians fight the French.

These English soldiers were fine to see. They marched across Virginia in bright red coats. They had many horses and wagons and guns. Their general, Edward Braddock, rode in a coach.

But these English soldiers did not know
the wilderness!

Washington told General Braddock they
could not take wagons into the wilderness. There were no roads. And those red
coats! The French could see them for
miles.

But Braddock would not listen to
Washington. "English soldiers always
wear red coats," he said. But he did leave
his coach behind.

The English went into the wilderness.
They cut down trees. They made roads.
Day after day, they pulled their big
wagons through the woods.

Then one day a terrible cry rang out.
It was Indians!

Behind every tree was an Indian or a

Frenchman in Indian dress. Indians were helping the French.

The French and the Indians shot at the English. They shot at their bright red coats. The English shot back, but they could not see the French and the Indians. They could see nothing but trees and smoke.

Washington fought hard for the English. But he could not help them. One by one, they died in their bright red coats. It was a terrible day in the wilderness.

The French had won a fight. But they had not won the war.

The king of England sent more soldiers to America. Soldiers from other colonies came to help the Virginia army. Indians began to help the English too. As time went by, the English got more and more Indians to help them.

There were more fights in the wilderness. There was fighting in Canada, too.

At last, in 1759, the English won a great battle in Canada. The "French and Indian War" was over. The English owned the wilderness at last.

George Washington had fought many times in this war. He showed that he was a brave soldier and a good leader.

Washington was made head of all the soldiers of Virginia. And he was chosen to help run the Virginia government.

6

WASHINGTON FINDS
A WIFE

The government of Virginia was in a town called Williamsburg. In Williamsburg, Washington met Mrs. Martha Custis.

Martha Custis was a young lady whose husband had died. Now she lived in Williamsburg with her two children, Patsy and Jack.

George Washington liked Martha

Custis. And Martha liked the tall young soldier. It was not long before they were married.

George Washington took his new family to live at Mount Vernon. He had much to do there.

There were 200 slaves to look after and many miles of land to farm. But Washington liked farming. He made Mount Vernon into one of the finest farms in Virginia.

Washington had many happy years with his family at Mount Vernon. Martha was a cheerful wife. And Washington loved little Patsy and Jack. Every year he sent to England for things for his farm. And he never forgot to send for toys for the children.

Washington needed many things from England. But as time went by, he found that it cost more and more to buy them. There was a new king in England. And this king put taxes on things the colonists needed. He told the colonists they must pay the taxes. He had wars going on all over the world. He needed the taxes to pay his soldiers.

Washington and other colonists did not want to pay these taxes. They stopped buying many things the king taxed.

7

ENGLISH COLONISTS AND AN ENGLISH KING

This new king of England was named George the Third.

George the Third thought he could use the colonies to get money for England. Other men in the English government thought so too. They made many new laws for the colonists. One of these laws made George Washington very angry.

The English had given away land in the West. They had given it to Washington's Virginia soldiers.

But then they made a law. The law took the land away again. This was too much for Washington!

Other colonists became angry in 1774. That year the English sent a ship full of tea to Boston. This tea was to be sold very cheaply. But only to a few men the English had chosen! Other colonists could

not buy tea for so little. They did not think this was fair.

One night some colonists dressed up like Indians. They went down to the ship. And they threw all the tea into the water.

People said these men had given the king a "Boston tea party."

Soon King George heard about the Boston tea party. He got very angry. He said no more ships could come to Boston until the lost tea was paid for.

The colonists thought the English had gone too far! Washington met with leaders from all the colonies. They talked about what should be done. The meeting was called the Continental Congress.

The Congress sent a letter to the king. They told him they wanted to make their own laws. They asked him to let ships come to Boston. King George did not listen to the Continental Congress.

8

FIGHTING IN LEXINGTON

King George sent soldiers from England. He sent them to make the colonists obey his laws.

But many colonists did not want to obey these laws. Boys in Boston made fun of the soldiers. They said they looked like lobsters in their bright red coats.

"Lobsterback! Lobsterback!" they would yell at the soldiers.

One day an English general learned that the colonists had guns in Lexington. Lexington was a little town near Boston.

On April 19, 1775, he sent his soldiers to get the guns.

But the farmers of Lexington knew the English were coming. On the night before, a man named Paul Revere had ridden all night on his horse to tell them. The English soldiers came. The colonists were standing in a line. They said they would not give up their guns.

Then somebody fired a shot. Was it a colonist? Or was it an English soldier? No one knows.

But there was fighting that day in Lexington. A war had started. A war between the English and the English colonists. This war would decide who would rule the colonies. Would it be the English king? Or would it be the colonists?

9

GENERAL WASHINGTON

Once again, the colonies sent their leaders to a meeting. And once again, George Washington met with the Continental Congress. This time he was dressed as a Virginia soldier.

The men at this meeting had much to talk about. The colonies were at war with England. The colonies needed an army—and they needed a general to lead the army.

"Who can be our general?" they asked.

A man named John Adams stood up to talk. "I have but one man in mind," said John Adams. "And that man is a gentleman from Virginia . . ."

The gentleman from Virginia was George Washington.

George Washington was now General Washington. He was head of all the soldiers from all the colonies. He was going to fight against the soldiers of his own English king.

This was hard for Washington to do. For 43 years he had been a good Englishman.

But Washington always did what he thought was right. And he felt he was right to fight the English. The English government had not been fair to the colonists.

In July of 1775, Washington took over his army in Boston. What an army it was!

There were boys from the farms. There were shopkeepers from the towns. There were men who had always lived in the wilderness. And there were Indians.

Some of these men were good fighters. But few had ever been soldiers. They did things no good soldier would do.

Men from one colony had fights with men from another. Boys went off to the woods and fired their guns for fun. Men

came when they wanted. They went home
when they wanted. Sometimes they took
things home that belonged to the army.

And these men did not even look like
soldiers. Many were dressed like farmers.
Some were even wearing the red coats of
English soldiers!

But this was not all. General Washington's men had few guns. And they had
little gunpowder. This was the army with
which Washington had to fight the
English.

10

A DECLARATION OF INDEPENDENCE

All that winter, George Washington worked to make his army strong. He trained his men to be soldiers. He sent away for gunpowder and guns. When spring came, Washington was ready to fight the English.

But the English were not ready to fight Washington. The English general,

William Howe, had to get food for his soldiers.

General Howe and his soldiers were in Boston. And in Boston there was no food for them to eat. Many of Howe's soldiers were dying of hunger. Others did not want to fight the colonists.

One spring day, Washington looked down from his hill over Boston. The English were sailing away.

No one knew where the English were going. But Washington knew that the English would come back one day. He thought they would come to the town of New York.

In the summer of 1776, he took his soldiers to New York.

In New York that summer, people were talking about a thing called independence. Some of the colonists were saying they did not want to be Englishmen anymore. They wanted their colonies to belong to them—not to England.

But many people did not want independence. A man in New York called these people "Sgnik Sdneirf." The Sgnik Sdneirf were "friends" of the English king.

Some of these "King's Friends" went back to England. But many stayed. They hoped the colonists would make friends again with their king.

But the Continental Congress was meeting in Philadelphia. They thought the colonies should not belong to England. On July 4 they decided to sign a "Declaration of Independence." And they decided to send it to their king.

"We are in a war for independence now," thought Washington. And he waited for the English to come.

11

THE BATTLE ON LONG ISLAND

Late that summer the English came back. They sailed up to Long Island in great warships.

The ships were carrying 20,000 soldiers! Not all of these soldiers were English. Some were Germans. England was paying them to help in the war.

General Howe had a strong army now.

He was ready to face George Washington.

One summer morning, the battle began. The English ships started to fire their guns. The 20,000 soldiers came onto Long Island. Washington and his men were there to meet them.

Washington put up a good fight. But by the end of a week he had lost 1,000 men. Soon, he thought, he would have no army left! He knew he must leave Long Island. He must take his men across the East River to New York.

Washington sent his men to get boats. When night came, they had all kinds of boats. They were ready to cross the river.

There was a fog that night. Howe's army did not see that Washington's men were leaving.

But someone saw Washington's men on the river. It was a woman. And this woman was a King's Friend. She did not want Washington's army to get away.

She sent her slave to tell the English. But her slave found German soldiers who did not speak English. They did not know what the slave was trying to say.

The English soldiers woke up the next morning. Washington and his men were gone. They had slipped away in the night.

12

WASHINGTON CROSSES THE DELAWARE

It was not long before the English came after Washington. There was another big battle in New York.

Once again, Washington lost many men. And once again, he slipped away.

Washington did not like to run away from the English. He wanted to fight. But Washington needed more soldiers. He knew he must wait until the colonies sent them.

All summer, the English chased after Washington's army. But they could not catch Washington. He and his men always got away.

In December, Washington came to Trenton, a town on the Delaware River. His men were dead tired. They had marched for miles. But Washington would not let them stop to rest. There were German soldiers close behind. He took his men in boats across the Delaware.

Soon these German soldiers came to Trenton. But they could not chase Washington across the river. Washington had taken every boat on the Delaware.

On Christmas night the German soldiers were in Trenton. They had good food to eat. They had wine to drink. They sat by their fires and sang.

But across the river, in George

Washington's camp, nobody sang. The men were tired and hungry and cold. "Will we ever win this war?" they thought. There seemed to be no hope.

But Washington had not given up. He had learned that the Germans were singing and drinking in their camp. "We will go back across the river," said

Washington. "We will catch the German soldiers."

Washington's men got into their boats. There were 2,500 soldiers, with horses and guns. They set out across the Delaware.

Far up the Delaware, the ice was breaking. Big cakes of ice came down the river. The soldiers were afraid the ice would hit the boats.

Many of the men turned back. But some went on. At three in the morning, they landed near Trenton. They marched to the German camp.

A shot was fired! The German soldiers ran for their guns. But there was no help for the German soldiers now. Washington's men were all around them.

Washington took 1,000 enemy soldiers that day. He had won a battle at last.

13

VALLEY FORGE

Washington had won a battle. But the English were still very strong. The next summer, Washington fought two battles against General Howe. Each time, Howe won.

When winter came, Howe took his soldiers to Philadelphia. George Washington had to find a camp for the winter too.

He took his men to Valley Forge. Valley Forge was an old iron forge near Philadelphia. Once men had made horseshoes and many other things at Valley Forge.

Now Valley Forge was only a name. It was the name of a hill by a river. There was no town on this hill. There were only a few farm houses and some trees.

It was raining when Washington came to Valley Forge. It was a sad army that marched up the hill in the rain. Their coats were in rags. Their shoes were worn out. Winter was coming. And they did not have houses to sleep in.

Washington had his men cut down trees. He had them put up houses.

It was cold that winter at Valley Forge. Inside their houses, men sat by their fires. Their eyes were red from the smoke. Outside, the men were freezing with cold. Their feet left blood on the snow. And the men had almost nothing to eat.

All winter, Washington wrote to the
Congress in Philadelphia. "Send food," he
wrote. "Send shoes. Send coats."

Congress sent food, but never enough.
It began to look as if the army would not
last until spring.

14

THE WAR ENDS

But at last spring came. And Washington still had an army. All through that terrible winter he had kept his men together.

And there was good news that spring. Up north, in Saratoga, some colonists had won a big battle. And Washington learned that French soldiers were coming to help the colonists. The French wanted England to lose the war.

Washington's men marched down the hill from Valley Forge. "This war will soon be over," they said.

But the war was not over so soon.

Washington still did not have enough soldiers to fight the English. Not many colonists wanted to be soldiers. Men went into the army in the winter. Then there were no battles. In the spring, they took their pay and went home.

Washington could not even get enough food or guns. Too many colonists were selling these things to the English.

For three years Washington worked to build his army. But in these three years the English won many battles.

An English general, Cornwallis, was down in the South. And he was winning fight after fight.

Then one day Washington got good

news. It was the best news he had had since the war began. French warships were coming to a town called Yorktown in Virginia. Cornwallis was going to Yorktown too. "Cornwallis is walking into a trap!" Washington thought.

Washington took his army to Yorktown. They fought Cornwallis from the land. French warships fought Cornwallis from the sea.

Cornwallis put up a good fight at Yorktown. But there was no way out for him. He was caught between Washington's army and the French.

On October 17, 1781, Cornwallis put up a white flag. His soldiers marched by Washington's men. His band played an English song. It was called "The World's Turned Upside Down."

The English put away their guns.

The war was over. The colonies had won their independence. At last they did not belong to England. A new country, the United States of America, was born.

15

NEW TROUBLES IN A NEW COUNTRY

Just before Christmas of 1783, George Washington said good-bye to his army.

For eight long, hard years he had led these men. Many soldiers had tears in their eyes as Washington said good-bye.

Then Washington rode off to his home, Mount Vernon. "I will rest," he wrote, "under my own vine and my own fig tree."

But there was not much rest for Washington. Many people came to Mount Vernon. Some came just to see the great man. Others came to ask his help. Things were not going well, they said.

The colonies were states now. They were united into one country, the United States of America. But no state did what was best for the whole country. Each state did what was best for itself.

The United States owed money to other countries. But the states would not pay the money. The United States needed an army. But the states would not send soldiers.

Congress tried to make the states do these things. But Congress was not very strong. Congress could not make the states work together.

The United States was like a family without a father.

Many Americans were troubled about

this. Some people even said that America should have a king. They wanted Washington to be the king of the United States.

But Washington did not want to be king. He did not want America to have a king. Washington thought that the people should choose their own leaders. Many wise men felt the same way.

16

PRESIDENT WASHINGTON

In May of 1787, Washington and some other men met in Philadelphia. They wanted to figure out a new way to govern their country.

For many months they worked hard. It was not easy to make a good plan. But Washington knew how to make men work together.

At last, there was a new plan for the government. It was called the Constitution of the United States of America.

The Constitution said many things about how the government should work. It said that each state would choose men for a new Congress. And these congressmen would make the laws.

The Constitution said that there should be one man at the head of the government. He was to be called the president.

People from every state would help choose him.

This was a new kind of government. It was to be a government "of the people, by the people, for the people."

Every state chose Washington to be the first president.

George Washington had many good men to help him run the country. For four years he worked with them to make America strong. They got money from the states. Now they could pay what was owed to other countries. They got soldiers for an army. They made many new laws.

It was hard to know what was best for the country. The men in the government did not always agree. But once again, Washington showed that he could make men work together.

At the end of four years he was made president again.

17

THE LAST YEARS

For four more years Washington led his country. Little by little, the states learned to work together. Little by little, the country grew strong. And little by little, Washington showed that the new kind of government worked.

Once again, the people asked George Washington to be president.

But Washington did not want to be president again. He was tired. He had done his best for his country, he said. He could do no more.

The people chose a new president. His name was John Adams.

George Washington went home.

Washington was 65 now. But he was still a strong man. He rode his horse. He looked after his farm. He went to parties and balls.

The months went by. They were happy months for Washington.

Then, one winter day, Washington caught a bad cold. The next day he was very ill. Two days later, on December 14, 1799, he died.

Washington was buried near his home at Mount Vernon. At last he could rest under his own vine and fig tree.

18

AFTER
GEORGE WASHINGTON

Just before Washington died, a new city was named. It was called Washington. It was to be the capital of the United States of America.

Soon towns all over the country were called Washington. People named their children Washington. There were songs about Washington and books about Washington.

Everyone told stories about the great man.

One story we all know.

One day, the story goes, George Washington took his hatchet. He cut down his father's cherry tree. His father was not pleased. He asked George if he did it.

"I can't tell a lie, Pa," said young George in the story. "You know I can't tell a lie. I did cut it with my hatchet."

"Run to my arms, you dearest boy!" cried his father.

This story comes from a book written after Washington died. Is it a true story? Probably not.

But everyone seems to have liked the story. It was told all over the world. People wanted their children to know that George Washington was a good man.

But Washington was more than just a good man. He was a great man and a brave man. All his life, he did what he knew he must. It often seemed as if he could not win. But he never gave up.

George Washington led his people in their war for independence. And he united them under one strong government.

That is why George Washington is called the Father of His Country.